A
DIFFERENT
WORLD

COLOR BLINDNESS

BY
ROBIN TWIDDY

KidHaven
PUBLISHING

Published in 2022 by
KidHaven Publishing, an Imprint of Greenhaven Publishing, LLC
353 3rd Avenue
Suite 255
New York, NY 10010

Edited by: John Wood
Designed by: Gareth Liddington

Cataloging-in-Publication Data

Names: Twiddy, Robin.
Title: Color blindness / Robin Twiddy.
Description: New York : KidHaven Publishing, 2022. | Series: A different world | Includes glossary and index.
Identifiers: ISBN 9781534538368 (pbk.) | ISBN 9781534538382 (library bound) | ISBN 9781534538375 (6 pack) | ISBN 9781534538399 (ebook)
Subjects: LCSH: Color blindness -- Juvenile literature. | Vision disorders in children-- Juvenile literature.
Classification: LCC RE921.T95 2022 | DDC 612.8'4--dc23

Printed in the United States of America

CPSIA compliance information: Batch #CSKH22: For further information contact Greenhaven Publishing LLC, New York, New York at 1-844-317-7404.

Please visit our website, www.greenhavenpublishing.com. For a free color catalog of all our high-quality books, call toll free 1-844-317-7404 or fax 1-844-317-7405.

Look out for these banners throughout the book to see how different people see the world.

KEY:

Red-green color blindness

Full-color vision

This book was written and designed with accessibility for people with color vision deficiency and dyslexia in mind.

Photo credits:

Cover & Throughout – CkyBe, Serhii Bobyk, Evgenii Emelianov, LauraKick, avian, Aleksandrs Bondars, 4&5 – ESB Professional, goir, 6&7 – galichstudio, FamVeld, 8&9 – Rio AbajoRio, paulaphoto, 10&11 – dezignor, d13, 12&13 – Victoria Shapiro, 14&15 – Farosofa, Phakamat BL, 16&17 – Kzenon, Germanova Antonina, Neveshkin Nikolay, VitaminCo, 18&19 – matimix, 20&21 – Dan Kosmayer, Sergey Novikov, 22&23 – Parilov, wavebreakmedia. Images are courtesy of Shutterstock.com. With thanks to Getty Images, Thinkstock Photo, and iStockphoto.

All facts, statistics, web addresses, and URLs in this book were verified as valid and accurate at time of writing.
No responsibility for any changes to external websites or references can be accepted by either the author or publisher.

CONTENTS

Words that look like <u>this</u> can be found in the glossary on page 24.

A DIFFERENT WORLD?

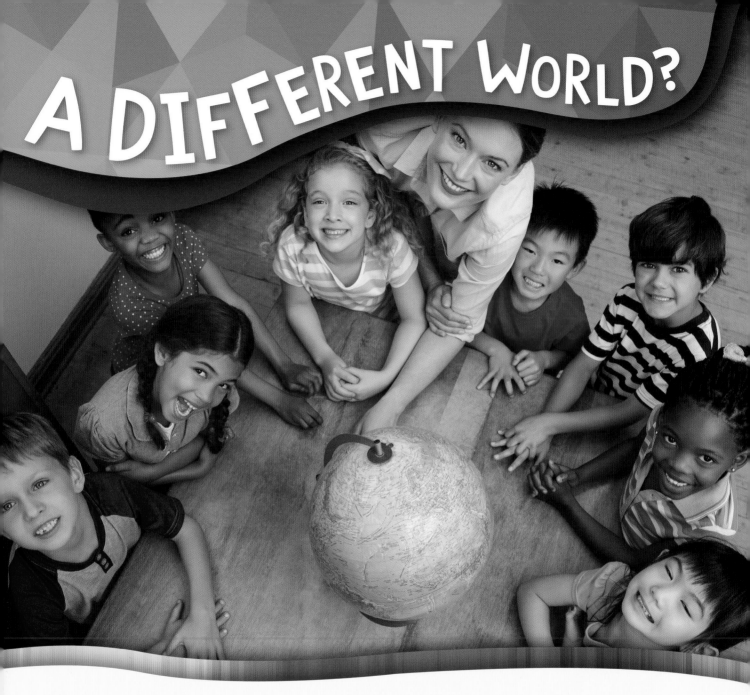

We all live in the same world, don't we? Well, for some people who have a <u>condition</u> known as color blindness, the world can look very different.

In this book you will have the chance to see what the world looks like for someone with color blindness. It is important to understand how others see the world and the challenges they face.

WHAT IS COLOR BLINDNESS?

A better term is color vision **deficient**, which just means a person sees fewer colors rather than not seeing any colors at all.

People with color blindness have eyes that work a little differently than other people's eyes. People with color blindness have trouble seeing some colors and mix others up.

6

Most people who have color blindness have the red-green type of color blindness, and most of them are male. Very few people have total color blindness. There are three types of color blindness:

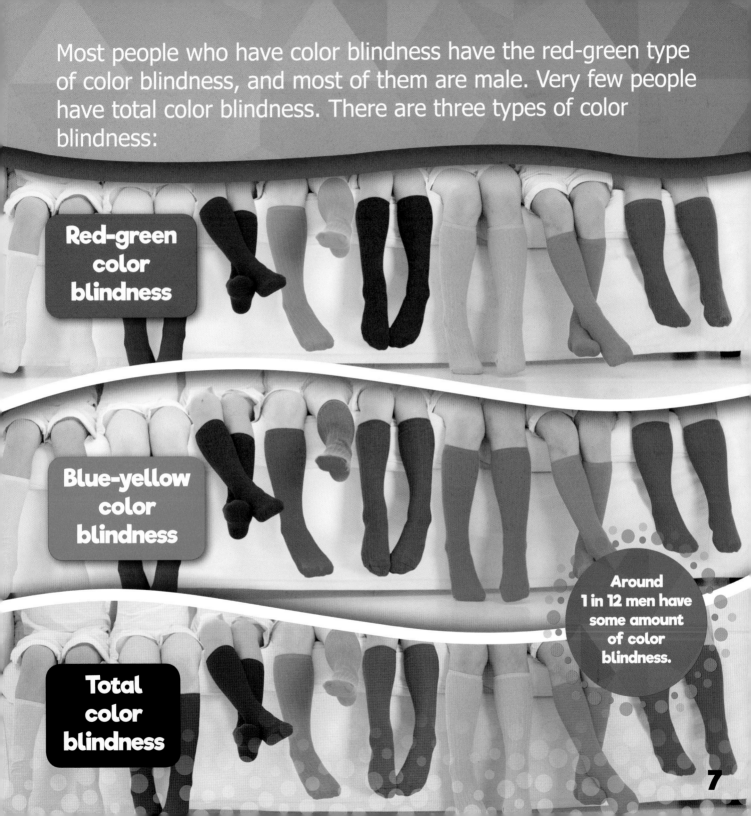

Red-green color blindness

Blue-yellow color blindness

Total color blindness

Around 1 in 12 men have some amount of color blindness.

7

RED-GREEN COLOR BLINDNESS

Any color can be made by mixing the three primary colors: yellow, red, and blue.

Full color wheel

Red-green color blindness color wheel

Even though it is known as red-green color blindness, many other colors are affected by it. Any color that is made by mixing red or green with another color will look different to someone with red-green color blindness.

If you have red-green color blindness, your eyes might have trouble seeing the color red or the color green. You might have trouble seeing both of those colors.

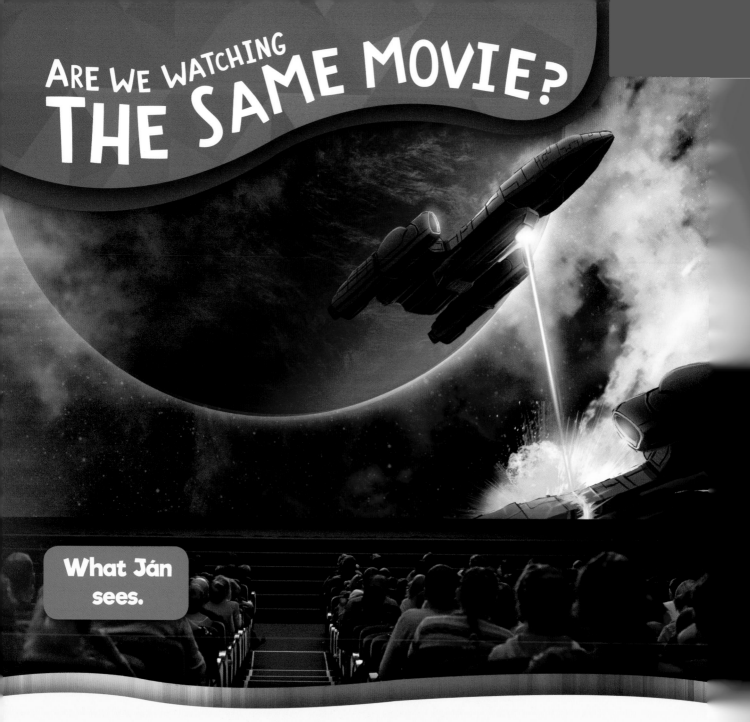

ARE WE WATCHING THE SAME MOVIE?

What Ján sees.

Adam and his best friend Ján love going to the movies. Adam has red-green color blindness and Ján does not. **10** Are they watching the same movie?

Adam has always had red-green color blindness, and the way he sees the world is normal to him. However, sometimes when he is watching a film, his color blindness can make it difficult to tell what is happening.

What Adam sees.

INSIDE THE EYE

The cone cells are switched on by different colors.

Inside our eyes are special things called cone cells. There are three types of cone cells, and each one helps us see a different color. One sees red, one sees green, and one sees blue.

The brain knows which color it is seeing by which cone cells are switched on. If the green cone cell isn't working, then the brain isn't told that it is seeing green.

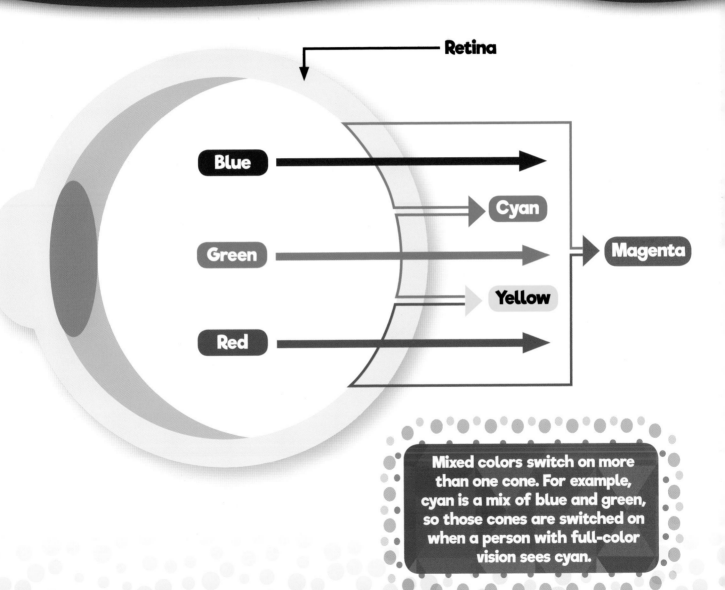

Retina

Blue

Cyan

Green

Magenta

Yellow

Red

Mixed colors switch on more than one cone. For example, cyan is a mix of blue and green, so those cones are switched on when a person with full-color vision sees cyan.

TELLING THE DIFFERENCE AT THE MARKET

For some people with red-green color blindness, it is hard to tell the difference between chocolate sauce and tomato sauce!

What Adam's dad sees.

Not being able to tell certain colors apart can sometimes make life tricky. When Adam goes to the market with his dad, Adam's color blindness makes it hard to tell which fruit is ripe.

Many fruits change color when they are ready to eat. Adam's dad doesn't have color blindness, so he knows that the yellow bananas are ripe and the green bananas aren't. Adam cannot tell which are green and which are yellow.

What Adam sees.

For Adam, all the bananas are yellow. Can you tell which bananas are ready to eat?

MADE WITH COLOR
BLINDNESS IN MIND

A lot of things in our world use color to tell them apart, such as the pieces in a board game, traffic lights, or buttons on a control pad.

Here are some examples of designs that help people with color blindness:

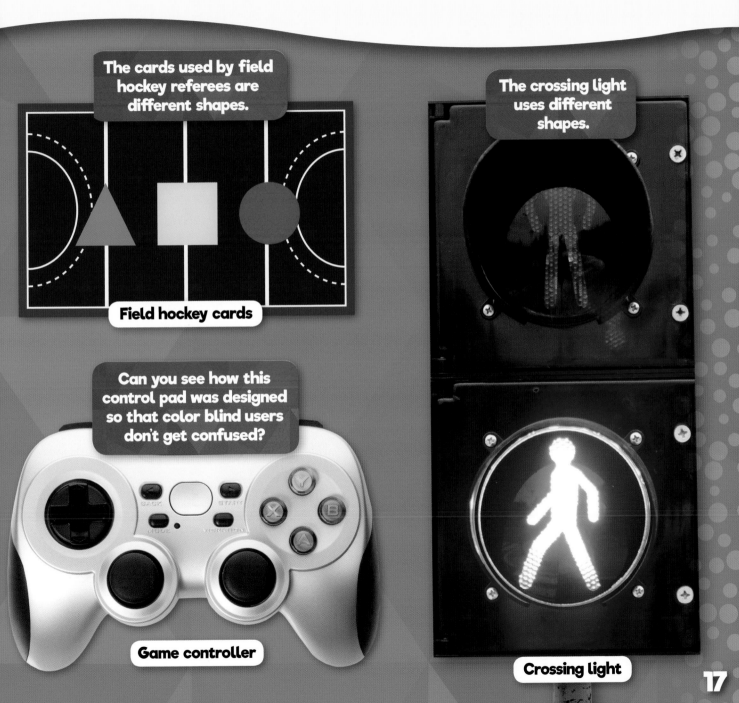

The cards used by field hockey referees are different shapes.

Field hockey cards

Can you see how this control pad was designed so that color blind users don't get confused?

Game controller

The crossing light uses different shapes.

Crossing light

WHICH TEAM?

What Adam sees.

Sometimes, when Adam plays soccer at school, it can be hard for him to tell who is on his team. He has to look really carefully to see the differences in the uniforms.

For the other players, it is really easy to tell who is on which team. Can you think of a way to make this match more <u>accessible</u> for people with color blindness?

What Ján sees.

Professional soccer clubs are now thinking about how to make games more accessible for people with color blindness.

OTHER TYPES OF COLOR BLINDNESS

This book has looked at what it is like to have red-green color blindness because most people who are color blind have some type of red-green color blindness, but there are other types.

Some people have blue-yellow color blindness, and some are completely color blind. Every person with color blindness sees the world a little differently. Many scientists believe that it is a little different for everyone.

SUPPORT

If you
think you
might have color
blindness, you should
talk to an adult.
They can help you
get a diagnosis.

If you have color blindness, you might need some support.
Adam's teacher supports him by having crayons that have
the color written on them. Adam's friend Ján helps him
when they are doing tasks in class.

Even though people with color blindness like Adam may see the world a little differently, we are more alike, all of us, than we are different.

GLOSSARY

accessible	being easily usable by people of different abilities
cells	the basic building blocks that make up all living things
condition	an illness or other medical problem
deficient	not having enough of something
designers	people who plan how something that is going to be made will look and work
diagnosis	a decision about what an illness or condition is
professional	having to do with a job that people who have special skills do
textures	the feel or appearance of objects' surfaces

INDEX